200+ Interview Q & A in Python Programming

99% Frequently Asked Interview Q & A

By Bandana Ojha

Introduction

The author of this book conducted so many interviews at various companies and meticulously collected all the important and frequently asked interview questions and answers with simple, straightforward explanations. Rather than going through comprehensive, textbook-sized reference guides, this book includes only the information required immediately to start his/her career as a python developer. Answers of all the questions are short and to the point. We assure that you will get here the 99% frequently asked interview questions and answers.

Good luck to ALL!!!

1. What is Python?

Python is a high-level, interpreted, interactive and object-oriented scripting language with threads, objects, modules, exceptions and the property of automatic memory management.

3. Who is the father of Python programming language?

Guido van Rossum , a Dutch programmer is known as the father of Python programming language.

3. How it got its name Python?

When Guido van Rossum began implementing Python, he was also reading the published scripts from "Monty Python's Flying Circus", a BBC comedy series from the 1970s. Van Rossum thought he needed a name that was short, unique, and slightly mysterious, so he decided to call the language Python.

4. What are the special features of Python?

Following are some of the salient features of python –

It supports functional and structured programming methods as well as OOPs.

It can be used as a scripting language or can be compiled to byte-code for building large applications.

It provides very high-level dynamic data types and supports dynamic type checking.

It supports automatic garbage collection.

It can be easily integrated with C, C++, COM, ActiveX, CORBA, and Java.

5. Differentiate between .py and .pyc files?

Both .py and .pyc files holds the byte code. ".pyc" is a compiled version of Python file. This file is automatically generated by Python to improve performance. The .pyc file is having byte code which is platform independent and can be executed on any operating system that supports .pyc format.

Note: there is no difference in speed when program is read from .pyc or .py file; the only difference is the load time.

6. What are the supported data types in Python?

Python has five standard data types –

Numbers

String

List

Tuple

Dictionary

7. How is python interpreted?

Python has an internal software mechanism which makes python programming easy. Program can run directly from the source code. Python translates the source code written by the programmer into intermediate language which is again translated it into the native language of computer. This makes it easy for a programmer to use python.

8. What is thread safety?

A function is said to be "thread safe" if executing it in multiple threads concurrently does not cause interactions between the threads. Architecturally this means that the function does not affect any variables accessible outside of the scope of a single call to the function. A function only modifies its own local variables and reference variables passed in from the calling scope.

9. What is functional programming?

Functional Programming is a coding style that focuses on defining what to do, instead of performing some action. Functional programming is derived from the mathematical style of thinking where you define the kind of inputs that go into a function and the kind of outputs that we can expect from the function. In functional code, the output of the function depends only on the arguments that are passed. Calling the function f for the same value of x should return the same result f(x) no matter how many times you pass it. Thus, it calls for a radically different style of thinking where you are rarely changing state. Instead of moving through steps, you think of data as undergoing transformations with the desired result as the end state.

10. What is the difference between @staticmethod and @classmethod in Python?

@classmethod: when this method is called, we pass the class as the first argument instead of the instance of that class (as we normally do with methods). This means you can use the class and its properties inside that method rather than an instance.

@staticmethod: when this method is called, we don't pass an instance of the class to it (as we normally do with methods). This means you can put a function inside a class, but you can't access the instance of that class (this is useful when your method does not use the instance).

11. What is generator in Python?

A generator in Python is a function which returns an iterable object. We can iterate on the generator object using the yield keyword. But we can only do that once because their values don't persist in memory, they get the values on the fly.

12. Why we use generators?

Generators give us the ability to hold the execution of a function or a step as long as we want to keep it.

13. When do you use generators in python?

Generators are useful when we don't want all the results and wish to hold back for some time.

Instead of using a callback function, we can replace it with a generator. We can write a loop inside the function doing the same thing as the callback and turns it into a generator.

We can replace loops with generators for efficiently calculating results involving large data sets.

14. What are closures in Python?

Python closures are function objects returned by another function. We use them to eliminate code redundancy.

15. What are Python decorators?

Decorators in Python are used to modify or inject code in functions or classes. Using decorators, you can wrap a class or function method call so that a piece of code can be executed before or after the execution of the original code. Decorators can be used to check for permissions, modify or track the arguments passed to a method, logging the calls to a specific method, etc.

16. What is string slicing in python?

The Python string data type is a sequence made up of one or more individual characters that could consist of letters, numbers, whitespace characters, or symbols. Because a string is a sequence, it can be accessed in the same ways that other sequence-based data types are, through indexing and slicing.

17. What is code profiling?

Code profiling is an attempt to find bottlenecks in your code. Profiling is supposed to find what parts of your code take the longest. Once you know that, then you can look at those pieces of your code and try to find ways to optimize it. cProfile, is an interface that mimics the profile module. Profiling code with cProfile is quite easy. All you need to do is import the module and call its run function.

18. How instance variables are different from class variables?

Instance variables: The variables in an object that have values that are local to that object. Two objects of the same class maintain distinct values for their variables. These variables are accessed with "object-name.instancevariable-name".

class variables: These are the variables of class. All the objects of the same class will share value of "Class variables. They are accessed with their class name alone as "class- name.classvariable-name". If you change the value of a class variable in one object, its new value is visible among all other objects of the same class. In the Java world, a variable that is declared as static is a class variable.

19. What is dictionary in Python?

The built-in datatypes in Python is called dictionary. It defines one-to-one relationship between keys and values. Dictionaries contain pair of keys and their corresponding values. Dictionaries are indexed by keys.

20. When do you use a dictionary instead of a list?

Dictionary is used when the data is labelled, i.e., the data is a record with field names.

Lists are better option to store collections of un-labelled items say all the files and sub directories in a folder. List comprehension is used to construct lists in a natural way. Generally, Search operation on dictionary object is faster than searching a list object.

21. How will you create a dictionary in python?

Dictionaries are enclosed by curly braces ({ }) and values can be assigned and accessed using square braces ([]).

22. What is Dogpile effect?

Dogpile effect is referred to the event when cache expires, and websites are hit by the multiple requests made by the client at the same time.

23. How can you prevent Dogpile effect?

This effect can be prevented by using semaphore lock. In this system when value expires, first process acquires the lock and starts generating new value.

24. What is NumPy?

NumPy is a Python package for scientific computing which can deal with large data sizes. It includes a powerful N-dimensional array object and a set of advanced functions.

25.Why NumPy is better than a List ?

Below are the reasons why NumPy is better than a List:

NumPy arrays are more compact than lists.

Reading and writing items is faster with NumPy.

Using NumPy is more convenient than to the standard list.

NumPy arrays are more efficient as they augment the functionality of lists in Python.

26. What are different ways to create an empty NumPy array in python?

There are two methods which we can apply to create empty NumPy arrays.

The first method to create an empty array.

import numpy

numpy.array([])

The second method to create an empty array.

Make an empty NumPy array

numpy.empty(shape=(0,0))

27. How can you share global variables across modules?

To share global variables across modules within a single program, create a special module. Import the config module in all modules of your application. The module will be available as a global variable across modules.

28. What is Web Scraping? How do you achieve it in Python?

Web Scrapping is a way of extracting the large amounts of information which is available on the web sites and saving it onto the local machine or onto the database tables.

To scrap the web: load the web page which is interesting to you. To load the web page, use "requests" module. parse HTML from the web page to find the interesting information. Python has few modules for scraping the web. They are urllib2, scrapy, pyquery, BeautifulSoap, etc.

29. What is a metaclass in python?

A metaclass is the class of a class. Like a class defines how an instance of the class behaves, a metaclass defines how a class behaves. A class is an instance of a metaclass.

A metaclass is most commonly used as a class-factory. Like you create an instance of the class by calling the class, Python creates a new class (when it executes the 'class' statement) by calling the metaclass. Combined with the normal __init__ and __new__ methods, metaclasses therefore allow you to do 'extra things' when creating a class, like registering the new class with some registry, or even replace the class with something else entirely.

30. What is Cython?

Cython is an optimizing static compiler for both the Python programming language and the extended Cython programming language (based on Pyrex). It makes writing C extensions for Python as easy as Python itself.

31.What is the purpose of Python startup environment variable?

Python startup contains the path of an initialization file containing Python source code. It is executed every time you start the interpreter. It is named as.pythonrc.py in Unix and it contains commands that load utilities or modify Python path.

32. What is a Class?

A class is a blue print/ template of code /collection of objects that has same set of attributes and behavior.

33. How do you create it in Python?

To create a class, use the keyword class with a class name beginning with an uppercase letter followed by a colon as follows –

class Employee:

34. Is there a difference between `continue` and `pass` in a for loop in python?

Yes, there is a difference. continue forces the loop to start at the next iteration while pass means "there is no code to execute here" and will continue through the remainder or the loop body.

35. What are Python Iterators?

Iterators in Python are array-like objects which allow moving on the next element. We use them in traversing a loop, for example, in a "for" loop.

Python library has a no. of iterators. For example, a list is also an iterator and we can start a for loop over it.

36. What are containers in Python?

Containers are data structures holding elements, and that support membership tests. They are data structures that live in memory, and typically hold all their values in memory, too. In Python, some examples of containers are:

list, deque, ...

set, frozensets, ...

dict, defaultdict, OrderedDict, Counter, ...

tuple, namedtuple, ...

str

37. What are the difference between iterable and iterator?

Iterable is an object, which one can iterate over. It generates an Iterator when passed to iter() method.

 Iterator is an object, which is used to iterate over an iterable object using __next__() method. Iterators have __next__() method, which returns the next item of the object.

Note that every iterator is also an iterable, but not every iterable is an iterator. For example, a list is iterable, but a list is not an iterator. An iterator can be created from an iterable by using the function iter(). To make this possible, the class of an object needs either a method __iter__, which returns an iterator, or a __getitem__ method with sequential indexes starting with 0.

38. What is a function call or a callable object in python?

A function in Python gets treated as a callable object. It can allow some arguments and also return a value or multiple values in the form of a tuple. Apart from the function, Python has other constructs, such as classes or the class instances which fits in the same category.

39. What is inheritance ?

Inheritance allows One class to gain all the members(say attributes and methods) of another class. Inheritance provides code reusability, makes it easier to create and maintain an application. The class from which we are inheriting is called super-class and the class that is inherited is called a derived / child class.

40. What are the different types of inheritance supported by Python?

These are the different types of inheritance supported by Python:

Single Inheritance – where a derived class acquires the members of a single super class.

Multi-level inheritance – a derived class d1 in inherited from base class base1, and d2 are inherited from base2.

Hierarchical inheritance – from one base class you can inherit any number of child classes

Multiple inheritance – a derived class is inherited from more than one base class.

41. How is Inheritance and Overriding methods are related?

If class A is a sub class of class B, then everything in B is accessible in /by class A. In addition, class A can define methods that are unavailable in B, and it can override methods in B. For Instance, if class B and class A both contain a method called func(), then func() in class B can override func() in class A. Similarly, a method of class A can call another method defined in A that can invoke a method of B that overrides it.

42. How would you define a protected member in a Python class?

By default, all methods and attributes in a python class are public. That means They can be accessed by the class members and by the module which contains its import.

__ can be used to define private attributes in a class. by default, we define all variable names as words, but if you define a class member starting with __ it becomes private and it cannot be accessed directly.

43. Can Python be compiled to machine code, C or some other language?

Cython compiles a modified version of Python with optional annotations into C extensions. Nuitka is an up-and-coming compiler of Python into C++ code, aiming to support the full Python language. For compiling to Java, you can consider VOC.

44. What are the advantages of immutable strings in Python?

There are several advantages.

One is performance: knowing that a string is immutable means we can allocate space for it at creation time, and the storage requirements are fixed and unchanging. This is also one of the reasons for the distinction between tuples and lists.

Another advantage is that strings in Python are considered as "elemental" as numbers. No amount of activity will change the value 4 to anything else, and in Python, no amount of activity will change the string "four" to anything else.

45. What are negative indexes in Python?

The sequences in Python are indexed and it consists of the positive as well as negative numbers. The numbers that are positive uses '0' that is uses as first index and '1' as the second index and the process go on like that.

The index for the negative number starts from '-1' that represents the last index in the sequence and '-2' as the penultimate index and the sequence carries forward like the positive number.

46. Why are negative indexes used?

The negative index is used to remove any new-line spaces from the string and allow the string to except the last character that is given as S[:-1]. The negative index is also used to show the index to represent the string in correct order.

47. How to retrieve data from a table in MySQL database through Python code?

import MySQLdb module as: import MySQLdb

establish a connection to the database.

db = MySQLdb.connect("host" =" local host", "database-user"="user-name", "password"="password", "database-name"="database")

initialize the cursor variable upon the established connection: c1 = db. cursor()

retrieve the information by defining a required query string. s = "Select * from dept"

fetch the data using fetch() methods and print it. data = c1.fetch(s)

close the database connection. db.close()

48. How instance variables are different from class variables?

Instance variables: are the variables in an object that have values that are local to that object. Two objects of the same class maintain distinct values for their variables. These variables are accessed with "object-name.instancevariable-name".

class variables: these are the variables of class. All the objects of the same class will share value of "Class variables. They are accessed with their class name alone as "class- name.classvariable-name". If you change the value of a class variable in one object, its new value is visible among all other objects of the same class. In the Java world, a variable that is declared as static is a class variable.

49. What is XML?

The Extensible Markup Language (XML) is a markup language much like HTML or SGML. This is recommended by the World Wide Web Consortium and available as an open standard.

XML is extremely useful for keeping track of small to medium amounts of data without requiring a SQL-based backbone.

50.When to use yield instead of return in Python?

The yield statement suspends function's execution and sends a value back to caller but retains enough state to enable function to resume where it is left off. When resumed, the function continues execution immediately after the last yield run. This allows its code to produce a series of values over time, rather them computing them at once and sending them back like a list.

51. What is pickling and unpickling?

Pickle module accepts any Python object and converts it into a string representation and dumps it into a file by using dump function, this process is called pickling. While the process of retrieving original Python objects from the stored string representation is called unpickling.

52. What are the tools that help to find bugs or perform static analysis?

PyChecker is a static analysis tool that detects the bugs in Python source code and warns about the style and complexity of the bug. Pylint is another tool that verifies whether the module meets the coding standard.

53. What is namespace in Python?

In Python, every name introduced has a place where it lives and can be hooked for. This is known as namespace. It is like a box where a variable name is mapped to the object placed. Whenever the variable is searched out, this box will be searched, to get corresponding object.

54. What is pass in Python?

Pass means, no-operation Python statement, or in other words it is a place holder in compound statement, where there should be a blank left, and nothing has to be written there.

55. What are the rules for local and global variables in Python?

Local variables: If a variable is assigned a new value anywhere within the function's body, it's assumed to be local.

Global variables: Those variables that are only referenced inside a function are implicitly global.

56. What is map function in Python?

Python map() function is used to apply a function on all the elements of specified iterable and return map object. Python map object is an iterator, so we can iterate over its elements. We can also convert map object to sequence objects such as list, tuple etc. using their factory functions.

map(function, iterable, ...)

We can pass multiple iterable arguments to map() function, in that case, the specified function must have that many arguments. The function will be applied to these iterable elements in parallel. With multiple iterable arguments, the map iterator stops when the shortest iterable is exhausted.

57. Does Python Support Object Oriented Scripting?

Python supports object-oriented programming as well as procedure-oriented programming. It has features which make you to use the program code for many functions other than Python. It has useful objects when it comes to data and functionality. It is very powerful in object and procedure-oriented programming when compared to powerful languages like C or Java.

58. Name the four main types of namespaces in Python?

Global,

Local,

Module and

Class namespaces.

59. How is memory managed in Python?

Memory management in python is managed by Python private heap space. All Python objects and data structures are located in a private heap. The programmer does not have access to this private heap. The python interpreter takes care of this instead.

The allocation of heap space for Python objects is done by Python's memory manager. The core API gives access to some tools for the programmer to code.

Python also has an inbuilt garbage collector, which recycles all the unused memory and so that it can be made available to the heap space.

60. Whenever Python exits, why isn't all the memory de-allocated?

Whenever Python exits, especially those Python modules which are having circular references to other objects or the objects that are referenced from the global namespaces are not always de-allocated or freed.

It is impossible to de-allocate those portions of memory that are reserved by the C library.

On exit, because of having its own efficient clean up mechanism, Python would try to de-allocate/destroy every other object.

61. Is python a case sensitive language?

Yes, Python is a case sensitive programming language.

62. How are arguments passed by value or by reference?

Everything in Python is an object and all variables hold references to the objects. The references values are according to the functions; as a result, you cannot change the value of the references. However, you can change the objects if it is mutable.

63. Explain how Memcached should not be used in a Python project?

Never use Memcached as the only source of the information you need to run your application. Data should always be available through another source as well

Memcached is just a key or value store and cannot perform query over the data or iterate over the contents to extract information

Memcached does not offer any form of security either in encryption or authentication

Memcached common misuse is to use it as a data store, and not as a cache

64. What is the difference between process and thread?

Both processes and threads are independent sequences of execution. The typical difference is that threads (of the same process) run in a shared memory space, while processes run in separate memory spaces.

65. How do you make 3D plots/visualizations using NumPy/SciPy?

Ans: Like 2D plotting, 3D graphics is beyond the scope of NumPy and SciPy, but just as in the 2D case, packages exist that integrate with NumPy. Matplotlib provides basic 3D plotting in the mplot3d subpackage, whereas Mayavi provides a wide range of high-quality 3D visualization features, utilizing the powerful VTK engine.

66. How can you share global variables across modules?

The canonical way to share information across modules within a single program is to create a special configuration module (often called config or cfg). Just import the configuration module in all modules of your application; the module then becomes available as a global name. Because there is only one instance of each module, any changes made to the module object get reflected everywhere.

67. What is the purpose of pass statement in python?

The pass statement in Python is used when a statement is required syntactically but you do not want any command or code to execute.

68. How to save an image locally using python whose URL address is already known?

We will use the following code to save an image locally from an URL address

1. import urllib. request

2. urllib.request.urlretrieve("URL", "local-filename.jpg")

69. What are the tools that help to find bugs or perform static analysis?

PyChecker is a static analysis tool that detects the bugs in Python source code and warns about the style and complexity of the bug. Pylint is another tool that verifies whether the module meets the coding standard.

70. Explain how Python does compile-time and run-time code checking?

Python performs some amount of compile-time checking, but most of the checks such as type, name, etc. are postponed until code execution. Consequently, if the Python code references a user -defined function that does not exist, the code will compile successfully. In fact, the code will fail with an exception only when the code execution path references the function which does not exists.

71. What is pylab?

A package that combines NumPy, SciPy and Matplotlib into a single namespace.

72. What are the best Python libraries for Machine Learning and Data Science?

Tensorflow, Numpy, Keras, Theano are the libraries for machine learning and data science.

73. What is the difference between NumPy and SciPy?

NumPy is a library for the Python programming language, adding support for large, multi-dimensional arrays and matrices, along with a large collection of high-level mathematical functions to operate on these arrays.

SciPy is a free and open-source Python library used for scientific computing and technical computing. SciPy contains modules for optimization, linear algebra, integration, interpolation, special functions, FFT, signal and image processing, ODE solvers and other tasks common in science and engineering.

74. What is the purpose of Python path environment variable?

It has a role similar to Path. This variable tells the Python interpreter where to locate the module files imported into a program. It should include the Python source library directory and the directories containing Python source code. Python is sometimes preset by the Python installer.

75. What is the purpose of Pythonstartup environment variable?

It contains the path of an initialization file containing Python source code. It is executed every time you start the interpreter. It is named as .pythonrc.py in Unix and it contains commands that load utilities or modify Pythonpath.

76. What is the purpose of Pythoncaseok environment variable?

It is used in Windows to instruct Python to find the first case-insensitive match in an import statement. Set this variable to any value to activate it.

77. What is the purpose of Pythonhome environment variable?

It is an alternative module search path. It is usually embedded in the Pythonstartup or Pythonpath directories to make switching module libraries easy.

78. What is the difference between deep and shallow copy?

Deep copy is used to store the values that are already copied. Deep copy doesn't copy the reference pointers to the objects. It makes the reference to an object and the new object that is pointed by some other object gets stored. The changes made in the original copy won't affect any other copy that uses the object.

Deep copy makes execution of the program slower due to making certain copies for each object that is been called.

Shallow copy is used when a new instance type gets created and it keeps the values that are copied in the new instance. Shallow copy is used to copy the reference pointers just like it copies the values. These references point to the original objects and the changes made in any member of the class will also affect the original copy of it. Shallow copy allows faster execution of the program and it depends on the size of the data that is used.

79. What is monkey patching in Python?

Monkey patching is a technique that helps the programmer to modify or extend other code at runtime. Monkey patching comes handy in testing, but it is not a good practice to use it in production environment as debugging the code could become difficult.

80. Explain about Python's parameter passing mechanism?

In Python, by default, all the parameters (arguments) are passed "by reference" to the functions. Thus, if you change the value of the parameter within a function, the change is reflected in the calling function. We can even observe the pass "by value" kind of a behavior whenever we pass the arguments to functions that are of type say numbers, strings, tuples. This is because of the immutable nature of them.

81. Explain "re" module in Python.

To modify the strings, Python's "re" module is providing 3 methods. They are:

split() – uses a regex pattern to "split" a given string into a list.

sub() – finds all substrings where the regex pattern matches and then replace them with a different string subn() – it is like sub() and returns the new string along with the no. of replacements.

82. Name few Python Web Frameworks for developing web applications?

There are various web frameworks provided by Python. They are web2py – it is the simplest of all the web frameworks used for developing web applications.

cherryPy – it is a Python-based Object-Oriented Web framework.

Flask – it is a Python-based micro-framework for designing and developing web applications

83. What is TkInter?

TkInter is Python library. It is a toolkit for GUI development. It provides support for various GUI tools or widgets (such as buttons, labels, text boxes, radio buttons, etc.) that are used in GUI applications. The common attributes of them include Dimensions, Colors, Fonts, Cursors, etc.

84. What is lambda function in python?

'lambda' is a keyword in python which creates an anonymous function. Lambda does not contain block of statements. It does not contain return statements.

85. What are help() and dir() functions in Python?

Help() and dir() both functions are accessible from the Python interpreter and used for viewing a consolidated dump of built-in functions.

Help() function: This function is used to display the documentation string and also facilitates you to see the help related to modules, keywords, attributes, etc.

Dir() function: This function is used to display the defined symbols.

86. What are the principal differences between the Lambda and Def?

def can hold multiple expressions while lambda is a uni-expression function.

def generates a function and designates a name to call it later. lambda forms a function and returns the function itself.

def can have a return statement. lambda can't have return statements

lambda supports to get used inside a list and dictionary.

87. Is Python platform independent?

No, Python is platform dependent.

There are some modules and functions in python that can only run on certain platforms.

88. Differentiate between append() and extend() methods.?

Both append() and extend() methods are the methods of list. These methods are used to add the elements at the end of the list.

append(element) – adds the given element at the end of the list which has called this method.

extend(another-list) – adds the elements of another-list at the end of the list which is called the extend method.

89. Explain about assert statement?

Assert statement is used to assert whether something is true or false. This statement is very useful when you want to check the items in the list for true or false function. This statement should be predefined because it interacts with the user and raises an error if something goes wrong.

90. Name the File-related modules in Python?

Python provides libraries / modules with functions that enable you to manipulate text files and binary files on file system. Using them you can create files, update their contents, copy, and delete files. The libraries are: os, os.path, and shutil.

Here, os and os.path – modules include functions for accessing the filesystem

shutil – module enables you to copy and delete the files.

91. What is JSON?

JSON(JavaScript Object Notation) is a lightweight data-interchange format that easy for to read and write. JSON is based on the JavaScript programming language. It is a text format that is language independent and can be used in Python, Perl among other languages. It is primarily used to transmit data between a server and web applications.

92. What are the data structure supported by JSON?

JSON supports two widely used data structures.

A collection of name/value pairs. This is realized as an object, record, dictionary, hash table, keyed list, or associative array.

An ordered list of values. This is realized as an array, vector, list, or sequence.

93. What does this mean: *args, **kwargs? And why would we use it?

We use * args when we aren't sure how many arguments are going to be passed to a function, or if we want to pass a stored list or tuple of arguments to a function.**kwargs is used when we don't know how many keyword arguments will be passed to a function, or it can be used to pass the values of a dictionary as keyword arguments.

94.What is Tuple?

A tuple is a collection which is ordered and unchangeable. In Python tuples are written with round brackets.

Example

Create a Tuple:

thistuple = ("Lotus", "Lilly", "Rose")

print(thistuple)

Once a tuple is created, you cannot change its values. Tuples are **unchangeable**.

95. What is the difference between tuples and lists in Python?

The main differences between lists and tuples are – Lists are enclosed in brackets ([ ]) and their elements and size can be changed, while tuples are enclosed in parentheses (( )) and cannot be updated. Tuples can be thought of as read-only lists.

96. What is composition in Python?

The composition is a particular type of inheritance Python. It means to inherit from the base class but form the relationship with the use of instance variables which are references to different objects. To demonstrate composition, we need to instantiate other objects in the class and then make use of those instances.

97. What is Flask ?

Flask is a small and powerful web framework for Python. It's easy to learn and simple to use, enabling you to build a complex, data-driven websites and web apps in a short amount of time.

98. What are the benefits of Flask?

Flask is part of the micro-framework which means it has little to no dependency on external libraries.

It makes the framework light while there is little dependency to update.

It has less security bugs.

99. Explain database connection in Python Flask?

Flask supports database powered application (RDBS). Such system requires creating a schema, which requires piping the schema.sql file into a sqlite3 command. So, you need to install sqlite3 command to create or initiate the database in Flask.

Flask allows to request database in three ways

before_request() : They are called before a request and pass no arguments

after_request() : They are called after a request and pass the response that will be sent to the client

teardown_request(): They are called in situation when exception is raised, and response are not guaranteed. They are called after the response been constructed. They are not allowed to modify the request, and their values are ignored.

100. What is the difference between Django, Pyramid, and Flask?

Flask is a "microframework" primarily build for a small application with simpler requirements. In flask, you must use external libraries. Flask is ready to use.

Pyramid are built for larger applications. It provides flexibility and lets the developer use the right tools for their project. The developer can choose the database, URL structure, templating style and more. Pyramid is heavy configurable.

Like Pyramid, Django can also use for larger applications.

101. What is Flask Sijax?

Sijax is nothing but a Python/jQuery library to make Ajax easy to use in web applications. Sijax uses JSON to pass data between the server and the browser.

102. What is the difference between "g" variable and "session" in the Flask?

"g" is data shared between different parts of the code base within one request cycle. For example, a database connection or the user that is currently logged in. While session provides you a storage place to store data for a specific browser. Which means using a specific browser, returns for more request.

103. How does a request context can be created in Flask?

A request context can be created by either

Automatically when the application receives a request

OR manually, by calling app.test_request_context ('/route?param=value)

104. How you can show all errors in the browser for the Flask?

To show all errors in the browser for the Flask, you need to run the Python file on the shell. The command used to see errors in detail is "app.debug = True".

105. How you can access sessions in Flask?

A session basically allows you to remember information from one request to another. In a flask, it uses a signed cookie so the user can look at the session contents and modify. The user can modify the session if only it has the secret key Flask.secret_key.

106. What does %r in python mean?

The 'r' in front tells Python the expression is a raw string. In a raw string, escape sequences are not parsed. For example, '\n' is a single newline character. But, r'\n' would be two characters: a backslash and an 'n'. Raw strings are handy in regex, in which the backslash is used often for its own purposes.

107. What is %S in Python?

Python has support for formatting any value into a string. It may contain quite complex expressions.

One of the common usages is to push values into a string with the %s format specifier. The formatting operation in Python has the comparable syntax as the C function printf() has.

108. What is GIL in Python?

Python supports GIL (the global interpreter lock) which is a mutex used to secure access to Python objects, synchronizing multiple threads from running the Python bytecodes at the same time.

109. What is PEP 8?

PEP 8 is a coding convention, a set of recommendation, about how to write your Python code more readable.

110. Name few Python modules for Statistical, Numerical and scientific computations ?

numPy – this module provides an array/matrix type, and it is useful for doing computations on arrays.

sciPy – this module provides methods for doing numeric integrals and solving differential equations.

Pylab – is a module for generating and saving plots

111. What is the common way for the Flask script to work?

The common way for the flask script to work is

-Either it should be the import path for your application

-Or the path to a Python file

112. What is docstring in Python?

A Python documentation string is known as docstring, it is a way of documenting Python functions, modules and classes.

113. What is the difference between a module and a library in Python?

A module is a file containing Python definitions and statements. The file name is the module name with the suffix .py appended.

A library is the collections of modules and sub modules.

114. What are the built-in types available in python?

Here is the list of most commonly used built-in types that Python supports:

Immutable built-in types of Python

Numbers

Strings

Tuples

Mutable built-in types of Python

List

Dictionaries

Sets

Dictionary

115. How will you convert a string to a frozen set in python?

frozenset(s) – Converts a string to a frozen set.

116. How can you pick a random item from a list or tuple?

choice(seq) – Returns a random item from a list, tuple, or string.

117. How will you remove all leading whitespace in string?

lstrip() – Removes all leading whitespace in string.

118. What is the output of [1, 2, 3] + [4, 5, 6]?

[1, 2, 3, 4, 5, 6]

119. How will you remove an object from a list?

list.remove(obj) – Removes object obj from list.

120. How will you get the index of an object in a list?

list.index(obj) – Returns the lowest index in list that obj appears.

121. How will you remove last object from a list?

list.pop(obj=list[-1]) – Removes and returns last object or obj from list.

122. How will you replaces all occurrences of old substring in string with new string?

replace(old, new [, max]) – Replaces all occurrences of old in string with new or at most max occurrences if max given.

123. How can you copy an object in Python?

To copy an object in Python, you can try copy.copy () or copy.deepcopy() for the general case. You cannot copy all objects but most of them.

124. How can you access a module written in Python from C?

You can access a module written in Python from C by following method,

Module ==PyImport_ImportModule("<modulename>");

125. How can the ternary operators be used in python?

The Ternary operator is the operator that is used to show the conditional statements. This consists of the true or false values with a statement that has to be evaluated for it.

Syntax:

The Ternary operator will be given as:

[on_true] if [expression] else [on_false]a, b = 10, 20big = a if a< b else b

Example:

The expression gets evaluated like if a<b else b, in this case if a<b is true then the value is returned as big=a and if it is incorrect then big=b will be sent as a result.

126. How to concatenate two strings in python?

In Python, there are a few ways to concatenate – or combine - strings. The new string that is created is referred to as a string object. Obviously, this is because everything in Python is an object – which is why Python is an objected-oriented language.

To merge two strings into a single object, you may use the "+" operator. When writing code, that would look like this:

str1 = "Hello"

str2 = "World"

str1 + str2

127. Can we concatenate one string and one integer together in python?

Python cannot concatenate a string and integer. These are considered two separate types of objects. So, if you want to merge the two, you will need to convert the integer to a string.

128. How can you check whether a data frame is empty or not?

The attribute df.empty is used to check whether a data frame is empty or not.

129. How to rename a file in python?

To rename a file,
use.os.rename(old_path,new_path).

130. How to generate random numbers in python?

The standard module random implements a random number generator. Usage is simple:

import random

random.random()

This returns a random floating-point number in the range [0, 1).

131. Which command do you use to exit help window or help command prompt?

Quit command is used. When you type quit at the help's command prompt, python shell prompt will appear by closing the help window automatically.

132. What is the syntax for list comprehension in Python?

The signature for the list comprehension is as follows:

[expression(var) for var in iterable]

For example, the below code will return all the numbers from 1 to 10 and store them in a list.

>>> alist = [var for var in range(1, 10)]

>>> print(alist)

133. What is the purpose of ** operator?

** Exponent – Performs exponential (power) calculation on operators. a**b = 10 to the power 20 if a = 10 and b = 20.

134. What is the purpose of // operator?

// Floor Division – The division of operands where the result is the quotient in which the digits after the decimal point are removed.

135. What is the purpose of is operator?

is – Evaluates to true if the variables on either side of the operator point to the same object and false otherwise. x is y, here is results in 1 if id(x) equals id(y).

136. What is the purpose of not in operator?

not in – Evaluates to true if it does not find a variable in the specified sequence and false otherwise. x not in y, here not in results in a 1 if x is not a member of sequence y.

137.What is the purpose break statement in python?

break statement – Terminates the loop statement and transfers execution to the statement immediately following the loop.

138. What is the purpose of continue statement in python?

continue statement – Causes the loop to skip the remainder of its body and immediately retest its condition prior to reiterating.

139.What is the purpose of pass statement in python?

pass statement – The pass statement in Python is used when a statement is required syntactically but you do not want any command or code to execute.

140. How will you convert a string to all lowercase?

lower() – Converts all uppercase letters in string to lowercase.

141. How will you get the max alphabetical character from the string?

max(str) – Returns the max alphabetical character from the string str.

142.How will you get min alphabetical character from the string?

min(str) – Returns the min alphabetical character from the string str.

143. How will you remove all leading and trailing whitespace in string?

strip([chars]) – Performs both lstrip() and rstrip() on string.

144. How will you change case for all letters in string?

swapcase() – Inverts case for all letters in string.

145. How will you get titlecased version of string?

title() – Returns "titlecased" version of string, that is, all words begin with uppercase and the rest are lowercase.

146. How will you convert a string to all uppercase?

upper() – Converts all lowercase letters in string to uppercase.

147. How will you check in a string that all characters are decimal?

isdecimal() – Returns true if a unicode string contains only decimal characters and false otherwise.

148. What is Python Set?

A set is a collection which is unordered and unindexed. In Python sets are written with curly brackets.

Example

Create a Set:

thisset = {"apple", "orange", "pear"}

print(thisset)

output is

{'orange', 'pear', 'apple'}

Note: the set list is unordered, meaning: the items will appear in a random order.

149.How will you check in a string that all characters are numeric?

is numeric() – Returns true if a Unicode string contains only numeric characters and false otherwise.

150. What is the difference between del() and remove() methods of list?

If you want to delete particular element whose index is unknown from the list use remove(element) and if you want to delete element at particular index use del(list[index]).

151. What are range() and xrange() in Python?

range() and xrange() are two functions that could be used to iterate a certain number of times in for loops in Python. In Python 3, there is no xrange , but the range function behaves like xrange in Python 2.If you want to write code that will run on both Python 2 and Python 3, you should use range().

range() – This returns a list of numbers created using range() function.

xrange() – This function returns the generator object that can be used to display numbers only by looping. Only particular range is displayed on demand and hence called "lazy evaluation".

152. Which one is more efficient range() or xrange()?

xrange() is more efficient because instead of generating a list of objects, it just generates one object at a time. Instead of 100 integers, and all of their overhead, and the list to put them in, you just have one integer at a time. Faster generation, better memory use and more efficient .

153. What is the difference between Accessor and Mutator method?

A method defined within a class can either be an Accessor or a Mutator method.

An Accessor method returns the information about the object, but do not change the state or the object.

A Mutator method, also called an update method, can change the state of the object.

154. What is the use of enumerate () in Python?

Using enumerate () function you can iterate through the sequence and retrieve the index position and its corresponding value at the same time.

155.What is abnormal termination?

The concept of terminating the program in the middle of its execution without executing last statement of the main module is known as an abnormal termination

Abnormal termination is undesirable situation in programming languages.

156. What are different methods to copy an object in python?

There are two ways to copy objects in Python.

copy.copy() function

It makes a copy of the file from source to destination.

It'll return a shallow copy of the parameter.

copy.deepcopy() function

It also produces the copy of an object from the source to destination.

It'll return a deep copy of the parameter that you can pass to the function.

157. What are exceptions in Python?

Python has many built-in exceptions which forces your program to output an error when something in it goes wrong. When these exceptions occur, it causes the current process to stop and passes it to the calling process until it is handled. If not handled, our program will crash.

For example, if function A calls function B which in turn calls function C and an exception occurs in function C. If it is not handled in C, the exception passes to B and then to A.

If never handled, an error message is spit out and our program come to a sudden, unexpected halt.

158. Why do we use Exceptions?

Exceptions not only help solve popular problems like race conditions but are also very useful in controlling errors in areas like loops, file handling, database communication, network access and so on. Exception handling is an art which brings you immense powers to write robust and quality code.

159. What are the optional statements possible inside a try-except block in Python?

There are two optional clauses you can use in the try-except block.

The "else" clause

It is useful if you want to run a piece of code when the try block doesn't create an exception.

The "finally" clause

It is useful when you want to execute some steps which run, irrespective of whether there occurs an exception or not.

160. What are most common exception errors?

IOError – It occurs on errors like a file fails to open.

ImportError – If a python module can't be loaded or located.

ValueError – It occurs if a function gets an argument of right type but an inappropriate value.

KeyboardInterrupt – It gets hit when the user enters the interrupt key (i.e. Control-C or Del key)

EOFError – It gets raised if the input functions (input()/raw_input()) hit an end-of-file condition (EOF) but without reading any data.

161. Is it mandatory for a Python function to return a value?

It is not at all necessary for a function to return any value. However, if needed, we can use None as a return value.

162. Does Python have a Main() method?

The main() is the entry point function which happens to be called first in most programming languages.

Since Python is interpreter-based, so it sequentially executes the lines of the code one-by-one.

Python also does have a Main() method. But it gets executed whenever we run our Python script either by directly clicking it or starts it from the command line.

We can also override the Python default main() function using the Python if statement.

163. What is Serialization?

Serialization is the process of transforming data structures or objects into a format that can be offloaded to a file, memory cache or transmitted over the network connection and the same object can be reconstructed later in the same or different environment.

164. What is unmarshalling?

The reverse process of rebuilding the object back from the stream of bytes is deserialization or unmarshalling.

165. How do we write a function in Python?

We can create a Python function in the following manner.

Step-1: to begin the function, start writing with the keyword def and then mention the function name.

Step-2: We can now pass the arguments and enclose them using the parentheses. A colon, in the end, marks the end of the function header.

Step-3: After pressing an enter, we can add the desired Python statements for execution.

166. What is a function call or a callable object in Python?

A function in Python gets treated as a callable object. It can allow some arguments and also return a value or multiple values in the form of a tuple. Apart from the function, Python has other constructs, such as classes or the class instances which fits in the same category.

167. What is Rstrip() in Python?

Python provides the rstrip() method which duplicates the string but leaves out the whitespace characters from the end.

The rstrip() escapes the characters from the right end based on the argument value, i.e., a string mentioning the group of characters to get excluded.

168. Why do you use the zip() method in Python?

The zip method lets us map the corresponding index of multiple containers so that we can use them using as a single unit.

169. How do you start a thread in Python?

To run a thread in Python, you need to call the following method of the thread module.

thread.start_new_thread (function, args[, kwargs])

170.What is Freeze?

Freeze make it possible to ship arbitrary Python programs to people who don't have Python. The shipped file (called a "frozen" version of your

Python program) is an executable, so this only works if your platform is compatible with that on the receiving end (this is usually a matter of having the same major operating system revision and CPU type).

171. What is the process of compilation and linking in python?

The compiling and linking allows the new extensions to be compiled properly without any error and the linking can be done only when it passes the compiled procedure. If the dynamic loading is used, then it depends on the style that is being provided with the system. The python interpreter can be used to provide the dynamic loading of the configuration setup files and will rebuild the interpreter.

172. How do you perform pattern matching in Python?

Regular Expressions/REs/ regexes enable us to specify expressions that can match specific "parts" of a given string. For instance, we can define a regular expression to match a single character or a digit .The Python's "re" module provides regular expression patterns and was introduce from later versions of Python 2.5. "re" module is providing methods for search text strings or replacing text strings along with methods for splitting text strings based on the pattern defined.

173. What is regular expression matching?

Short for regular expression, a regex is a string of text that allows you to create patterns that help match, locate, and manage text.

174. Is regex case sensitive?

By default, Symantec Messaging Gateway treats regular expressions as case-insensitive. However, you can use a special string to toggle case sensitivity to a different mode. You can switch your regular expression query from case-insensitive to case-sensitive as many times as you want.

175. When would you use triple quotes as a delimiter?

Triple quotes """" are string delimiters that can span multiple lines in Python. Triple quotes are usually used when spanning multiple lines or enclosing a string that has a mix of single and double quotes contained therein.

176. Explain the use of break and continue in Python looping.

The break statement stops the execution of the current loop. and transfers control to the next block. The continue statement ends the current block's execution and jumps to the next iteration of the loop.

177. What is multiprocessing?

Multiprocessing allows you to create programs that can run concurrently (bypassing the GIL) and use the entirety of your CPU core. Though it is fundamentally different from the threading library, the syntax is quite similar. The multiprocessing library gives each process its own Python interpreter and each their own GIL.

178. How is Python thread safe?

Python ensures safe access to threads and completely thread safe. It uses the GIL mutex to set synchronization. That is because the Python GIL (Global Interpreter Lock) prevents multiple native threads from executing Python bytecodes at once.

179. How a Python program or component is tested?

Python comes with two testing frameworks.

The doctest module searches for pieces of text that look like interactive Python sessions,

and then executes those sessions to verify that they work exactly as shown

The Python unit testing module, sometimes referred to as "PyUnit," is a Python language version of Junit. PyUnit supports test automation, sharing of setup and shutdown code for tests, aggregation of tests into collections, and independence of the tests from the reporting framework.

180. What is the command to debug a python program?

The following command helps run a Python program in debug mode.

$ python -m pdb python-script.py

181. Name few methods that are used to implement Functionally Oriented Programming in Python?

filter() – enables you to extract a subset of values based on conditional logic.

map() – it is a built-in function that applies the function to each item in an iterable.

reduce() – repeatedly performs a pair-wise reduction on a sequence until a single value is computed

182. How Python supports encapsulation with respect to functions?

Python supports inner functions. A function defined inside a function is called an inner function, whose behavior is not hidden. This is how Python supports encapsulation with respect to functions.

183. What happens in the background when you run a Python file?

When we run a .py file, it undergoes two phases. In the first phase it checks the syntax and in the second phase it compiles to bytecode (.pyc file is generated) using Python virtual machine, loads the bytecode into memory and runs.

184. What are the basic Data Types Supported by Python?

Numeric Data types: int, long, float, NoneType

String: str

Boolean: (True, False)

NoneType: None

185. What do you mean 'call by value'?

In call-by-value, the argument expression is evaluated, and the result of this evaluation is bound to the corresponding variable in the function. So, if the expression is a variable, a local copy of its value will be used, i.e. the variable in the caller's scope will be unchanged when the function returns.

186. What do you mean 'call by reference'?

In call-by-reference evaluation, which is also known as pass-by-reference, a function gets an implicit reference to the argument, rather than a copy of its value. As a consequence, the function can modify the argument, i.e. the value of the variable in the caller's scope can be changed.

187. What is ELIF statement in Python?

The ELIF statement allows you to check multiple expressions for TRUE and execute a block of code as soon as one of the conditions evaluates to TRUE.

Similar to the else, the ELIF statement is optional. However, unlike else, for which there can be at most one statement, there can be an arbitrary number of ELIF statements following an if.

188. Can we use 'else' statement with 'for loop' in Python?

In most of the programming languages (C/C++, Java, etc.), the use of else statement has been restricted with if conditional statements. But Python allows us to use the else condition with for loops. The else block just after for/while is executed only when the loop is NOT terminated by a break statement.

189. How do you open an already existing file and add content to it?

In Python, open(<filename>,<mode>) is used to open a file in different modes. The open function returns a handle to the file, using which one can perform read, write and modify operations.

Example:

```
F = open("simplefile.txt","a+") #Opens the file in
append mode

F.write("some content")   #Appends content to
the file.

F.close()   # closes the file.
```

190. What mode is used for both writing and reading in binary format in file?

"wb+" is used to open a binary file in both read and write format. It overwrites if the file exists. If the file does not exist, it creates a new file for reading and writing.

191.How to do file operation in python?

Python provides the open() function for all file operation such as read, write, update, delete.

fileObj = open (<file-name>, <access-mode>, <buffering>)

few <access-mode> examples:

r   → opens file for read only mode

r+ → opens file for both read and write

w   → opens file for write only

a   → opens file in append mode

code example:

Open the file

fileObj = open("Test.txt","r")

```
  if fileObj:

    print("Successfully opened the file")
```

#Close the file

fileObj.close()

C:\Users\Python>py Test.py

Successfully opened the file

192.Why are local variable names beginning with an underscore discouraged?

Because they are used to indicate a private variable of a class. As Python has no concept of private variables, leading underscores are used to indicate variables that must not be accessed from outside the class.

193. How error is handled in python?

The error handling is done using exceptions that are caught in try blocks and handled in except blocks. If an error is encountered, a try block code execution is stopped and transferred down to the except block.

In addition to using an except block after the try block, you can also use the finally block.

The code in the finally block will be executed regardless of whether an exception occurs.

```
try:

   #block of code
```

    except Exception1:

        #block of code

    except Exception2:

        #block of code

    #other code

194. How to send email using Python?

Python **smtplib** module can be used to send mail using SMTP.

```
import smtplib

smtpObj  =  smtplib.SMTP(  [host  [,  port  [,
local_hostname]]] )
```

Here is the detail of the parameters –

host – This is the host running your SMTP server. You can specify IP address of the host or a domain name like tutorialspoint.com. This is optional argument.

port – If you are providing host argument, then you need to specify a port, where SMTP server is listening. Usually this port would be 25.

local_hostname – If your SMTP server is running on your local machine, then you can specify just localhost as of this option.

195. How to use Python in doing DB operation?

Sample Code:

```python
import mysql.connector

  # Creating DB connection
dbConn = mysql.connector.connect (
    host = "server",
    user = "user123",
    passwd = "pwd123",
    database = "myDB"
    )
# Creating cursor
dbCursor = dbConn.cursor()
try:
    # Get data from Table
    dbCursor.execute("select * from myTable")
    # Get the rows
    rows = dbCursor.fetchall()
    for record in rows:
        print(record);
```

except:

   dbConn.rollback()

dbConn.close()

196. Explain Lambda function with detail example?

Python creates anonymous function (without 'def') which can accept any number of arguments but can return only one value in the form of expression.

It is similar to C/C++ inline function but not exactly same.

Syntax:

Lambda arguments expression

Example 1:

```
x = lambda x: x + 5
print ("(x+5) = ",x(20))
C:\Users\Python>py Test.py
(x+5) =  25
```

Example 2:

```
avg = lambda x,y: (x + y)/2
print ("average(x+y) = ",avg(10,20))
```

C:\Users\Python>py Test.py

average(x+y) = 15.0

197. How to create PDF file using Python?

First you have to install the utility **PyFPDF** which is **FPDF for Python.**

C:\User\Python>python -m pip install fpdf

```
from fpdf import FPDF

pdf = FPDF()

pdf.add_page()

pdf.set_font("Arial", size=15)

pdf.cell(150, 15, txt="PDF Created from Python !!!", ln=1, align="C")

pdf.output("Test.pdf")
```

198. How to read and extract Compressed files?

```
# import module

from zipfile import ZipFile

# zip file name

file_name = "Test.zip"

# opening the zip file in READ mode

with ZipFile(file_name, 'r') as zip:
```

```python
# print contents of the zip file

zip.printdir()

# extract all files

print('Extracting all the files now...')

zip.extractall()

print('Done!')
```

```
C:\Users\Python>py Test.py
```

File Name	Modified	Size
file.txt	2019-02-07 17:19:58	15
Test.py	2019-02-07 22:44:40	411
Test.txt	2019-02-07 17:17:02	15

Extracting all the files now...

Done!

199. What are the ways of doing GUI Programming in Python?

Python provides various options for developing graphical user interfaces (GUIs). Most important are listed below.

Tkinter – Tkinter is the Python interface to the Tk GUI toolkit shipped with Python.

wxPython – This is an open-source Python interface for wxWindows

JPython – JPython is a Python port for Java which gives Python scripts seamless access to Java class libraries on the local machine

200. How to create a simple http server using Python?

```python
from http.server import HTTPServer, BaseHTTPRequestHandler

class SimpleHTTPRequestHandler(BaseHTTPRequestHandler):

  def do_GET(self):

    self.send_response(200)

    self.end_headers()

    self.wfile.write(b'Hello, world from Python Http Server !')

httpd = HTTPServer(('localhost', 8888), SimpleHTTPRequestHandler)

httpd.serve_forever()
```

Hello, world from Python Http Server !

201. How to do logging in Python?

Python uses "logging" module and have exhaustive set of methods to configure and log at various log level as shown in below example:

```python
import logging

logging.basicConfig(
    filename='example.log',
    level=logging.INFO,
    format='%(asctime)s  :  %(levelname)s  -> %(message)s'
    )

logging.debug("This is a debug log")

logging.info("This is an info log")

logging.warning("This is a warning log")

logging.error("This is an error log")

logging.critical("This is a critical log")

C:\Users\Python>type example.log
```

2019-02-08 11:28:23,808 : INFO -> This is an info log

2019-02-08 11:28:23,809 : WARNING -> This is a warning log

2019-02-08 11:28:23,809 : ERROR -> This is an error log

2019-02-08 11:28:23,809 : CRITICAL -> This is a critical log

Please check this out:

Our other best-selling books are-

500+ Java & J2EE Interview Questions & Answers-Java & J2EE Programming

200+ Frequently Asked Interview Questions & Answers in iOS Development

200 + Frequently Asked Interview Q & A in SQL , PL/SQL, Database Development & Administration

100+ Frequently Asked Interview Questions & Answers in Scala

100+ Frequently Asked Interview Q & A in Swift Programming

100+ Frequently Asked Interview Q & A in Cyber Security

Frequently asked Interview Q & A in Java programming

Frequently Asked Interview Questions & Answers in J2EE

100+ Frequently Asked Interview Questions & Answers in Android Development

Frequently asked Interview Q & A in Angular JS

Frequently asked Interview Q & A in Database Testing

Frequently asked Interview Q & A in Mobile Testing

Frequently asked Interview Q & A in Test Automation-
Selenium Testing

Frequently   asked Interview Questions & Answers in
JavaScript

200+ Frequently Asked Interview Questions &
Answers in Manual Testing

Interview Q & A series-9
200+
Interview Q & A in
iOS Development
Objective-C
Swift
Programming
By Bandana Ojha

Interview Q & A Series-16
100+ Interview Q&A
in Cyber Security
Data Security
Information Security
Bandana Ojha
90% Frequently asked
Interview Q&A

Interview Q & A Series -15
Android
Development
Frequently Asked
Interview Q & A

Interview Q & A series -11
100+ Frequently Asked
Interview Q & A
in Swift
Programming
Bandana Ojha

Interview Q & A Series-13
100+ Frequnetly asked
interview Q & A in
Database
Testing

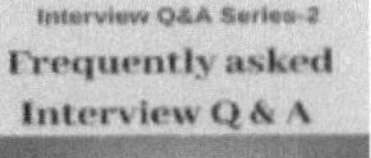

Interview Q&A Series-2
Frequently asked
Interview Q & A
Test Automation
Selenium Testing
By Bandana Ojha

Interview Q & A Series -3
Frequently Asked
Interview Q&A
in Mobile Testing
iOS
By Bandana Ojha

Interview Q & A Seies-6
Frequently Asked
500+ Java & J2EE
Interview Q & A
J2EE
Java
Java JSP Servlet EJB JMS
JDBA JNDB
By Bandana Ojha

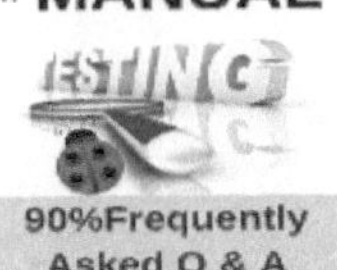

Interview Q & A series -1
200+
Interview Q & A
in MANUAL
TESTING
90%Frequently
Asked Q & A

Interview Q & A Series - 14
100+ Interview Q & A
in
Angular JS
A
90% Frequently
Asked Q & A

Interview Q & A Series - 8
100+ Frequently asked
Interview Q & A in
Scala
Scala Programming
By Bandana Ojha

Interview Q & A Series -14
Interview Q & A In
JS
JavaScript
90% Frequently asked
Interview Q & A
By Bandana Ojha

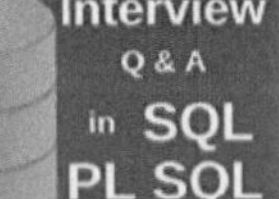

Interview Q & A Series -12
200+
Frequently asked
Interview
Q & A
in SQL
PL SQL
DATA BASE
Development & Administration
Bandana Ojha

Interview Q & A Series -4
Frequently asked
Interview Q& A in
Java
Java
By Bandana Ojha

Interview Q & A Series -7
200+
Interview Q & A
in Python
99% Frequently Asked
Q & A
Bandana Ojha